terse

terse verse

anne mcmanus

SINCLAIR-STEVENSON

details

several universities
and skid row
sums it up
I'm afraid

oh . . .
and getting laid

First published in Great Britain by
Sinclair-Stevenson Limited
7/8 Kendrick Mews
London SW7 3HG England

Copyright © 1992 by Anne McManus

British Library Cataloguing in Publication Data
A CIP catalogue record for this book is available from the British Library.

ISBN: 1 85619 178 8

Typeset by Rowland Phototypesetting Limited,
Bury St Edmunds, Suffolk

Printed and bound in Great Britain by
Biddles Ltd, Guildford, Surrey

CONTENTS

finding form

tried a novel
found a hovel
of boys' own prose
dilatory doze
of narrative
couldn't grovel
chose a poem
instead
not as good
as yours
of course
but written
smitten
by clauses
pauses
new

no more
closed doors
like you
trapped
in inherited
language
bondage
when you
don't own
the sources

spice

triste

devastating
while we're mating
all bereft
when you've left
returning to
your higher things
importances
that manhood brings

run

fight back
lady
he's only a hack
learning the rules
crown jewels
of kingship
and domination
abomination
hit and run
find the sun
it's waiting
baiting
you free
like me
see
so easy
when you know
how
now

sanity

when I went off my head
you said
it's all to do
with fear and dread
of sexuality
I listened too
and in your bed
I followed meekly
where you led
solving my lunacy
by surrender
to your gender
you my mender
phallic sender
of sanity

I snuggled up
but shook my head
it wasn't true
the more I read
the problem was
you

visit

come to call
have you
come to shatter
my peace again
come to water
my stall
smother
my call
doesn't matter
my pain
at all
my relentless
rainfall
does it
you gain
sanctity
maul
haul
yourself
to sanity
have yourself
a ball
standing tall
while I
fall
foul

curse

calling it
a cunt's
an affront
bugger
mugger
how do you
like
swearing
back
hack
from
her
bearing
malice
too
coo
you hate it
cock
well
here
I'll sock
it
to
yer
sir
big
illiterate
adulterate
ultimate
voyeur

ego

build a legend
over there
all the fans
stand and stare
at your masculinity
your absolute divinity
your bristling sensitivity
see if I care

doggo

with your sneers
and jeers
and slapping me down
you make me feel
like a demented Yorkshire Terrier
yapping and snapping
round the heels
of a languid big Dalmatian
ridiculous
absurd
but irrepressible
with the daftest feminist rapping
you ever heard
trying to change your spots
there's no dignity
in this relationship
we must rearrange
stop the rot
graduate at least
to Scottie and Alsatian

Scotties go
for the jugular

tired

you can shove off
mate
decorate
another gate
blister
another sister
but it's late
mister
and I hate
that spate
that puts folk
down

encounter

grim
prim
tight narrow mouth
set
ready
you
encounter
turd of
uncouth youth
surly sexy
sturdy
sinning
winning smile
lusty guile
craft
acting daft
flexes muscles

you tussle and fail
with your reflexes
complexes
and grin

space invader

if you live with me
you'll take away
my creativity
longevity
self respect
time for reflection
you can't help it
your big important
ego
inevitably
flows over
and
eats up the air
the places
no time to stare
into space
you want your
dinner
supper
subservience
audience
playmate
soul saver
waitress on the psyche
poor suffering man
at the top of the tree
of academe
famous
deconstructive
destructive
superstar
there are others
better by far

qualified
to buttress and butter
you up
and lie every day
but I dry up
and slowly die
it's happened before
and I was reborn
but only just
don't trust
my chances
again
you won't take less
then
such wise men
of no compromise
goodbye
and amen

promise

woe
to the foe
of women
I say
you'll undergo
trimmin
a certain way
without delay
when we win
the day
ball breaking
is taking
the easy
way out
you'll have to pay
shaking
and yelling
and total hell belling
wouldn't like
to sell
you
short
the way you
fought
all those years
you deserve
a worthy adversary
a proper
gob stopper
of peer
power
in your final
hour

hilarity

nasty bitched up
feminist
disposition
never smiles
just wallows
in wily intuition
well
what's so funny
anyway
sonny
with you
in view
if you move over
a bit
the shit will clear
from my vision
I'll cheer up
too

retreat

the powerful men
are the most interesting
but full of stress
and bless you with it
push it on you
and their shit too
avoid
the horrid
lot of 'em

mums and dads

you're wanting mother
like most of them do
but I'd rather
have father
than all that
palaver
and playing wet nurse
again
to any more men
there are so few
mature ones
around

renegade comrade

the bearer of a higher
consciousness
you think
personal love
has no right
to exist
it is flawed
by living
but pious cant
and circumstance
do not excuse
your real abuse
of life
this way

otherwise
surprise
wise guy
I agree
fearless
in our theory
to discover
with the other
more than lover
a way to be

addicted

thrill me
fill me
instil me
with love
and heaven above
then leave me
alone
moaning
groaning
only
loaning
you
no
don't phone
don't shove
your holiness
at my lowliness
you've been
and gone
it's done
you won
so
roam
along
revolutionary
rolling
stone

compartments

you've had
your ration
of passion
for today
he said
enthusiastically
donning his jeans
and scenes
of outside worlds
unfurled
proud plumage
of little boys
and petty ploys
rummaging in
resistance to
this offering
proffering
of peace within

within
whither
where
daring
caring
sharing
even
beyond your
ken
men
of war

revolutionary

another
preachy poem
from the front
today
oh brother
you still
have your say
teaching others
far away
willing lovers
have to pay
scorning
safer days
smothering
any other
way
but yours
applause
cause
for guilt
without
delay

regret

you've gone then
in a hurry
flurry
of words
misheard
at the time
no sign
you meant it
spent it
in rhyme
and worry
vented
sublime
sorry

apology

offended
distended
with hurt
at dirt
you think
I wrote
about you
old softy
heart sinking
after all
my god
I'm sorry
don't worry
didn't think
you'd break
forsaking
that pinnacle
miracle
always
of strength
disdaining
lengths
of lovers
revealed
congealed
your brittle
spittle
but trusting
lusting
was never
my way
do say
it's OK
eh

enough

liberated
are we fated
to get dated
madly mated
never sated
yet again
prisoners of
every slob
who comes
to pay
his disrespect
his fond neglect
comes
to say
look at mine
it's bigger
life giver
grave digger
nay lad
take your prick
away

cynic

blurt
your squirt
this way
any day
I'll hurt
you back
later

discovery

all these men
who need
women
who need
only themselves
to discover
not lonely
these shelves
of recovery
for us
take your fuss
elsewhere
don't care
must delve
aware
you stare
dumbfounded
at our
resounding
lack of need
for your
sustenance
romance
merry dance
our discontent
venting
greed
for our own
culture
you
glaring
vultures
at our

ruptures
all that
nurture
now the future
this time
no
nursery rhyme

no

forgiving me
for living
again Hercules
are you
unchaining
my mission
to serve thee
with permission
hardly new
but screw
yourself
this time

growing

weaving
fantasy
evading
your
reality
lack of
mutuality
imposing my
definition
of the
situation
freely

romantic

go away
so I can dream
about you
machinate
and scheme
around you
our lives
interwoven
you've chosen
me
dreams
seem wetter
don't hurt
and fetter
not curt
much better
all round

sceptic

give me a ring
one day
we'll have a fling
don't lay
bets on it
though

repose

resting
after
nesting
doing some
infesting
inspecting
infecting
impregnating
me
mating me
and mixing up
my fate
again
just testing
if I've changed
at your behest
rearranged
in context
fatal challenge
amen

struggle

shambling
rambling
but no denying
I'm trying
ambling
fumbling
rumbling
suffering
and sampling
your way
power
sour
but near

illusion

male heroics
female stoics
balls and bounce 'em
never trounce 'em
lovely prick
wild and thick
orgasm
simple spasm
muscular
that's all
what gall
to fathom
coital bliss
naught amiss

escape

thin lips
derision
cruel quips
collision
twixt
mixed sexes
complexes
reflexes
a–quiver

deliver
perfection
genuflection
woman
summon
servility
bow to my
gentility
come here
I can sneer
better
leer
wetter
feeling fear
nearby

don't sigh
deny
his lie
untie
the knot
beat the rot
clot
fly

redundancy

I'll spank you
if you
wank again
Henry
is that
the thanks
I get for
hankering
after you
cantankerous
fool
home made
mule
self serving
pool
on the floor
endless bore
what's a whore
for
then

bored

go away
and display
your proud peacock
plumage
elsewhere
I've had more than
my share
of any
of it

drawbridge

why am I truly
only
happy
when alone
no wonder
the way
you men
plunder
my strength
my life
my vitality
take it away
for yourselves
and I'm on
my strong shelf
recovering
again

web

insistent
wrangling
tangling
my existence
resistance
wangling
me
free from your
persistent
stranglehold

intrusion

I love my life
and wouldn't change it
who are you
to rearrange it

rationalise

a forlorn feature
of that
crazed creature
man alive
is his strive
to arrive
at clarity
of his stale
reality
of his male
virility
of his cool
civility
taking
faking
making
mockery
of every
female
wail
and drive

warning

heed
a love
that goes
with you
this day
growing
overflowing
in wondrous ways
it needs
watering
though
not slaughtering
slowly
by holy cant
pomposity
and neurotic greed

cold

there's a
dearth
of worth
round here
I fear
since you
came near
all
sneering
discontent
resentment
malcontent
at living
giving
affection
it might
mean
loss of grace
weaken your
case
imply
embrace
couldn't
face that
could you

nocturne

dreamt about you
last night
we were having
a grand old
fight
all that might
and posturing
worshipping
our roles
own goals
poor souls
nightmare
of frustration
indignation
wild
gesticulation
no celebration
or wet theme
at all

game

regular regret
don't fret
I'll bet
you met
your match
a catch
all set
to whet
your appetite
for fight
a sight
begetting
rights
of way

growth

taming me
is laming a
free
spirit
and I won't have
it again
from
any more men
it's finally
amen

ideal

you would have to be
kind and caring
not
bold and daring
staring
flaring
your nostrils
posturing
daily
baring teeth
sharing grief
false belief
sparing nobody

see me

melancholy
but jolly
if you'll
mollify
glorify
how I try
every day
another way
to say
no way
for men
to lay
slay
betray
underpay
another
hen
own goal
after all

unfamiliar

it's like
a woman you know
very well
stealing away
in the night
on some knowing
needing flight

what right
do you have
to question
her plight
her sudden
new
urgent
motives

learn

there's method
in my madness
irrevocable
sadness
gladness
get in harness
man
I'm your fan
when we've cured
your span

handsome ransom

I wish somebody would
defile
your grand
profile
while I
wait
and see
what you do
then
God of men
when
human qualities
trivial jollities
fun frivolities
evade
your masquerade
your defiance
of reliance
on inner depths
renegade

absolution

while meek
we are
bleak our star
seek afar
solution
but revolution's
pure ablution
mending
sending
liberation
sanitation
validation
until then
men can
fend
for themselves

altered angle

watching you
watching my
misdirection
imperfection
everywhere
bad selection
crude collection
don't stare
dare you
to care
instead
defy you
to classify
my head
shedding
your sighs
in bed
your whys
coming too
new ties
breaking through
old lies
ringing
true

flouncing off

nice little nightcap
of a vicious self-deceiving
authoritarian
invading
my space
disgraceful
why am I here
won't be
no fear
for long
and you can go
play strong
games
and heroes
with somebody else
and leave me alone
with my unplugged phone
inaccessible
safe
hidden
and free

glimpsing the game

I sometimes smile
at you
put on a happy face
and all the while
thinking
without blinking
what a vicious
disgraceful viper
you are
needing to wipe the floor
with everyone
you meet
in case they defeat
you first
it's all power
and position
this mission
of yours
to prove yourself
but all closed doors
on development
contentment
fulfilment
and peace
what do you prove
with shoving
and shouting
and clouting people
constantly
except how
weak
and bleak
these goals

you seek
and utterly
inhuman

but you know that one
and smile back
meekly . . .
for a moment

rocky road

just supposing
your self-loathing
equalled mine
we'd be fine
sunshine
everywhere
sharing
our despair
rare
solidarity
daring them
to enter
our venture
in mutuality
sensitivity
twin tense
proximity
mocking
the fair
and sane
out there
to rain
disdain
on them
who dare
proclaim
they're sane
without
despair

usurper

monopoly
of history
deadly poisonous
fantasy
invader
masquerader
parader
of superiority
can't fool
me

disillusion

steady trickle
of snide asides
what a pickle
to deal in lies
feeble fickle
your ploy defies
all attempts
to rationalise
analyse
empathise
you paltry prickle
you energise
and tickle
my sympathies
only

ball game

sexy sod
playing god
randy rod
aping rambo
full of macho
carrying women
over your
shoulder
much bolder
now older
are you
dropping them
as well
oh hell
now you're trussed
I'm concussed
banging head
hangover
no clover
no lover
either
wiser
though

achievement

I just want my peace
today
release
away
from you
driven
riven
workaholic
never resting
always testing
yourself
stop interfering
with me
I'll go at my pace
there's no race
I'll frolic
and be free

pattern

you're all bent
with disapproval
do relent
I meant
well

'reality'

afterwards
when you see
how much they hurt
you dismiss your
endless criticisms
and dirt
as witticisms
designed only
to convert
people who need it
to 'reality'
a desperate
conjectured
fatality
dreamed up
and schemed up
by you
to compensate
for your own burning
self loathing

but supposing
these people
can see
their reality
very well
and don't want
yours
at all
and in the end
just want
you
to go away

and play
your sadistic
games
elsewhere
over there
dare you see
this –
your
reality

downer

feeling great
today
energy
on display
till I came
your way
hearing
you say
happiness
must pay

stern stuff

told
my pompous
husband
he took himself
too seriously
he thought it was
a compliment
talk about
crossed wires
tame sires
lame
dire
admirers
of solemnity

geology

solid rock strata
up your garter
know what you're after
grafter
granite intrusion
what an illusion
dolomite
fighting
inside me
hiding real
lack of lust
for trusting
contact
hard fact
of life
wife

escape

twitching with remorse
as marriage took
its lonely course
eventually
I found resource
demanding
a divorce
from futile days
suburban ways
a boozy haze
the violent phase
that so amazed
the neighbour's gaze
the dreaded stays
of wifely things

success

I kept telling him
warning him
yelling
if you push me
into straight society
it'll kill me
I don't fit
can't cope
with routine
and discipline
but still he wasn't
listening
as I fell
fell
fell
and fractured into
jagged bits
he just hit out
even more
shouting about
failure
and snail's pace
people
who mess up
the race
for success

but
it's not defeat
to refuse
to compete
is it

72

fragile

alone
in the splendour
of my female
gender
tense
independence
rendering me
ill at ease
doing all
I please
without saluting
your highfalutin
knowledge
dull porridge
diet of stew
marital glue
all behind
I'm finding it
delicate
predicating
my life
entirely
on me
your wife
no longer
stronger
mustn't flee
from the
sensation
elation
incantation
frail
but
free

ex

proud professor
student blesser
cool assessor
of lesser
mortals
in scientific
portals
with technocratic
chortles
that maim

sole possessor
of knowledge
what garbage
when we know
whose glow
life flow
kept you going
knowing
fame
would come

gets lonely
up there
men only
beware
down here
only blame
awful shame
very lame
too tame
insane

refrain

you're promising
somebody else
the earth
again
but it's
all in vain
worth nothing
your money
your power

it's the daily
accumulating
hurts
and humiliations
that drive women
away
one day
they up
and run
and must have sun
at last
be fun
be free
now listen to me
this time

hangover

I have tremendous
anger
towards you
stored up inside
I've been hoarding it
for thirteen years
and now my fears
about the consequences
prevent me releasing it
so I still have the anger
but frustration too
and sometimes it's so tight
a little knot
growing bigger and bigger
that I fight hard
with it or
it will explode
entirely
a fire
a holocaust
an eruption
of grief
of anger
of despair
at the way
you beat me
defeated me
utterly
and left me for
dead
it's all still
unsaid
and unsolved

unresolved
can you ever be free
either
and whole
till it all
comes out
but that would
mean
obscene
doubting of
yourself on
such a profound
level
the devil
himself
couldn't cope
with your wrath
I certainly can't
so I remain
silent
venting it
inwards
as usual
but it's eating
me
defeating me
again
I must
go
away
soon
soon
soon
or this second honeymoon
is over
for ever

an ex's reflexes

you've gone too far
with the grandma
stuff
it's too rough
too tough
I have sensitivities
you know
it jars now
OK we know the score
rubbed in
hammered home
you don't need to go on
about sagging tits
and low bums
and surgical repair jobs
blobby
and slobby women
of a certain age
it's outrage
these insults
who the hell are you
anyway
adonis
reborn
or something
so you don't
fancy me
any more
it's only
a bore
what's a whore
for

then
all lonely
when
there are these opportunities
for importunities
and invention
and attention
to detail
it's a waste
and bad taste too
your preference
for young ones
when the old
and wise
can play
a few surprises
any day
anyway
the reluctance
is mutual
so we'd better stay
frigid and dry
while life
floats away
passes by
and doesn't come
this way
again
no sigh
or why
just amen
and glum goodbye

. . . vindication

what would you do
if GRANDMA
was a star
one day
growing tall
just like you
through writing
and resting
and being still
in her small humble nest
fulfilling a need
not fighting
and killing
and greed
for glory
showing her way
her story
was best
after all . . .

out of touch

there's a human quality
that you
know nothing at all
about
you're so blind
to *kindness*
simple kindness
responding to need
and smallness
with all your tallness
you could afford
to bend
to lean
to give
to someone feeling
small
but instead
you invariably
take the opportunity
to make them smaller
even blame them
for being small
in the first place
your trampling
superhero
philosophy
despising weakness
but so weak yourself
which is the mainspring
of your cruelty
but proving you're strong
all the time
by failing to respond

to human need
is so wrong
so misconceived
you're bleeding away
your life blood
and all you've achieved
is ashes
if you deny
your basic human seed

inwards

you need some inner peace
to release you
from all this tension
not to mention
releasing me too
from malice
of all those
poseurs
who don't accept
themselves
and need to project
to protect
and hide
that wide yawning
abyss
inside
that divided room
a vacuum
a chasm
with spasms of fear
and futility
and nakedness
making you mean
and defensive
and hurting
and full of shit
instead of admitting
you're small
and frightened
and empty
and filling the space
and beckoning hole
with humility

and honesty
and grace
and reckoning
with your past
at length
at last
and ultimately

free

got out of that whole
rigmarole
of me and you
and who's who
today
who'll pay
who'll say
sorry
don't worry
bolted
my hole
my goals
now

vice

write-off

what a shock
to see you
they said you were dead
that's what they told me
they all said so
you were
going down slow
rotting
hopeless
gone too far
such a shame
I blamed your marriage
of course
that awful divorce
no inner resources
but here you are
better than ever
and I thought you were
finished
over
I know
there's a point
of no return
isn't there?

where?
a lot you know

tipple

booze
you use
me
ever
never
enough
too
tough
sleeping
rough
though
you
must
go
now

phoenix

utter
flutter
of total
exhaustion
extortion
of sanity
possible
so massive
action
traction
swimming
winning
back
energy
sanctity
vanity
even
self respect
to reflect
no neglect
these days
new ways
pay investment
in health
wot wealth
waiting
there
all
the time

gasping

I came up for air
from the gutter
for a while
staring
baffled
at the styles
the temperaments
everyone venting
some kind of paranoia
on the other
the nearest
no dearest any more
just trample
and hurt
dismantle
oh brother
this dirt
is killing you
suffocating your
spirit
you're willing
it
too

guilt

top up
stop up
life force
silly
girl
new course
quite frail
in the gale
of remorse

tut

sick of bending
to other people's
wills
sick of sending
apologetic
notes
begetting
votes
for wrecking
someone's
tranquil
evening
hit the ceiling
that night
what swill
wanting to kill
me
for minor
indiscreet
confession
obsession
oh dear
really don't
fit the bill

courage

we all have our
weaknesses
hidden
bleaknesses
that suddenly
wreak havoc
seeking
retribution
freaking out
our usual
solid
contribution

don't be afraid
only man
was made
maverick
slick
prick
clever dick
free of doubt
full of clout
that's what this
is all
about

false dichotomy

stealthy
underminer
of health
this wealth
of self
perusal
refusal
to confront
society
history
mystery
just
navel
gazing
fazing
dazing
in hazy
morbid
introspection
self
reflection
need
injection
of perspective
in my
digestion
daily
hailing
once again
external
struggle
or does it
start
here

ride

come on
an alcoholic
frolic
with me
we'll see
who lasts
longest
strongest
in blasphemy
epitome
of false
heroics
stoics
only
in tranquillity
of total
amnesia
seizure
of false
power
an hour
of glory
forgery
a story
of vanity
insistent
sanity
it appears
till fears
take over
and we
shudder
again
always

need
more
and then
close
the door
my friend
on humanity

daze of tranx and roses

tranquillisers
dull despisers
of life
strife
housewife's
appetisers
frowners
downers
drowning
joy
ploys
to keep us
numb
dumb
womb tied
truth plied
cripples
ripples
only
lonely
silent thorns
prickling
tickling
not tearing
us apart
no heart
in it
at all
what gall
this sapping
mapping
our wifely road

scared

drifters
dopers
profound
no hopers
mopers
not coping
at all
fall
somewhere
else
sort
yourself
away
from
here
my fear
my dear
is stealth
of experience
endangering
my health

lecture

now
haven't they told you
it's OK
for men to get
as drunk
as skunks
macho
rambo
glow
for wimmin
it's sinnin
though
get that clear
my dear
and we'll go
far
my jars
only

con

fighting
the battle
against
cup addiction
vile affliction
only in fiction
does this
benediction
inspire
what liars
they've been
these mean
obscene
bottles

judgment

self-destruction
they smugly say
pushing on
their certain way
masochism
they decide
rushing on
their safety ride
weary rhythm
witticism
criticism
false pride
bleary prism
makes me hide
stigmatism
I deride
whose side
are you
on

hopeless

the saga
of lager
bears repeating
lonely meeting
false greeting
no heating
on the bottle
sudden throttle
wax audacious
raucous
coarse
and crude
vulgar
lurid
very rude
brilliantly
lewd
where's our
cautious
friendship
now
well oiled
we foiled
nicety
despising
certainty
relishing our
gaiety
spontaneity
frailty
us boozers
all losers
terminal

refusers
human
excuses
all these
abuses
no uses
at all

secret

back from the brink
with drink
you think
I'm a sober
member
of society
phobic
about
notoriety
if only
you knew
you'd spew
your solid
respectable
guts
and very few
endearments
would remain

sage

going to hell's
an oil well
I recommend
if you manage
to come back
see the hacks
still poised
little boys
proud plumage
testy tonnage
what courage
you'll have
to send them
packing

misfit

I've graduated
from gutter slut
I now have a hut
I call home
no longer to roam
the streets again
defeated
cheated
chapped
and chafing
listening always
to other folk
laughing
enjoying life
being hubby and wife
and happy family

no longer homeless
yet ill at ease
even now
it's the times
I'm allergic to
and money lust
all around
the sound of
clanking clunking
counting money
and inter-continental
thankyous
for handouts
screaming shouting
gime
gime

more
more
mean
ugly
a whoredom
for a queendom
it's become

I'd rather be
a bum
and lie low

woe

utter bliss
on the piss
all you miss
is history

slices of life

outside

don't
fit the bill
never will
bitter pill

. . . still

expression

it's not that I object
to penetration
but I don't like being
fucked
when reading
so I'm pleading
plucking at
a different way
of writing
from hard tight
punch packed
crunch cracked
prose
with its
clipped
tight lipped
certainties
its mean keen
jawlines
and masculinist
brutalism
a futilism
of smash and grab
and plunder
and tear asunder
I want to wonder
and hesitate
and be baffled
not waffle
exactly
but vague
in vogue
in print

114

in flow
and out of prison
where you have to
know

corsets

men need to hold on
to traditional forms
to button up
tighten in
emotions
corset
dangerous feelings
or else they might
flow all over
molten
moist
glowing
erupting
disrupting
slowing
the nice neat
drum beat
of status quo

timeless

it's dated
they all say
about my kind of writing
fated
we don't want any '68
streams of consciousness
we're not interested
in dreams
those old fashioned themes
of sanity
and madness
we just want to celebrate
money
and gladness
for today
go away
with your blackness
the sun is shining
its milk and honey
what's wrong with you

so I slink off
hurt
bewildered
suppressed rage
a creature from
another age
a season
when reason and passion
held sway
or seemed to
but now they hate
all mention

of doubt
and criticism
so I'm relegated
to historic relic
staying derelict
for ever

never pays
predicting fate
though

vampire

I need space for writing
you said
and I thought for a while
here's the perfect man
who'll respect
my need for writing
who'll understand
stupid
romantic
fool that I am
you meant moving in on mine
and owning that
too
pissing round its corners
territory new
like dogs do
except that they feed
on tinned food
usually
not fresh female flesh
and life blood
and it's true
you hide away
and sleep all day
waiting for
inspiration
and wake up thirsty
but my work
comes first
as well
so how about a fix
of crucifix
and blessing

yes
hell
is the place
to write
your bestseller

record

writing
articles
particles
of the story
only
phoney
distortions
contortions
abstractions
a fraction
of glory
sections
selections
vivisections
flashing
erections
bashing
rejections
dashing
reflections
a sudden
potent
moment
of history

sister

'too intelligent'
the magnificent comment
of a publisher
recently
your book is just too
intelligent
to sell
well well
I said
I know women intellectuals
aren't exactly
well represented
but bloody hell
this is so low
and cunning
and ambivalent
I can't take it in

till
resentment sets in
when I see
it's a woman

politicise

suburban
lady
novels
even
ad feminem
are gems
only
of precious
little
non
concerns
trivial
turns
no scars
at all
no
real fall
from Hampstead
grace
turn your
face
towards
Kilburn
rats burn
there
you'd learn
to stare
and blow
your fiona
ruthie
cassandra
love
affair
terminally

fuel

tension
mother of
invention
what they never
mention
when teaching you
to write

no sell-out

desperate tedium
of happy medium
will plague you
all your days
unless
you raise
hell

home

god
what a hell hole
north London is
full of festering
rancid Trots
of yesteryear
predatory dykes
coming too near
wonder why
I live here
must be my fear
of normality

natural

how folk like to cluster
making a fuss
wanting to speak
be spoken to
they huddle
and cuddle
and follow me
desperate to escape
from them
be free
alone
not natural
see

alone

what the hell is it
with these people
they can't leave
a person
alone
a solitary soul
seems a threat
to them
especially wet
bedraggled
in pain
in the rain
you don't know
how my heart's
singing
inside
but I'm not wide
open
for invasion
persuasion
pity
want to hide
from the shitty
gregarious
human race
predatory
waiting
knowing what's
best for me
hate it
detest its
nosiness
in every public place

128

turn my face
away
from it
yet still
they pursue
a person alone
a woman alone
enigma
yoohoo
yoohoo
don't be sad
and alone
as though the words
go to gether
like you all
together
haven't you heard
me
I'm shrieking
my message
to men
to them all
this is my stall
my space
the few inches
around me
not a sound please
in my ear
pushing
intruding
poking
prevailing
I sail a lonesome
little boat
these days
but it is afloat

129

so merrily
inside
I'm hiding my
happiness
from you
in case you take it away
again
all men do
doesn't make it less
not at all
just warm and safe
and true to its owner
this loner
means it
believe me
so leave
me
alone

red plastic

you know how divorced women
are an underclass
all on their own
taking a nosedive
in standard of living
unless he's of a giving
disposition

well I don't have
the right kind of plates
anymore
don't have to worry
about losing it
abusing
my possession of shit
position
of hausfrau

no now I have another kind
of plastic
fun merry
very bad taste
no more wasted
hours
polishing the silver
in one room
dusting pine in another
no I can indulge
my true lebenslust
trust my passion
for the unfashionable
the kitsch
with a kitchen

gleaming with bright
red beaming plastic
shod
you would call it
dear absent
god

sigh

why
do those we cherish
just perish
and wither
and die
like the others

lament

I've been up all night
wild eyed
frightened
that you died
can't comprehend
a world without you
first boyfriend
romance
merry dance
godsend
to carry me through
traumas
teenage years
all those fears
of being on earth
you told me
I was worth it
deserved to be
can't see you again
so big and strong
and handsome
and gone gone gone
where've you gone
without me
what's it like
why didn't I know
you were going
could have helped you
saved you
stopped you
given you strength
this time
like you gave me

and confidence
you've no business
dying
without letting me
know
I could have showed
you
how my new middle class world
wasn't worth it
wasn't a patch
on the warmth
and love
of you
back then
now I'm just another
rootless cosmopolitan
without a past
like I dreamt of being
when I had you
my last few roots
all straggling
on the surface
while you lie
snuggled up
underneath
a damned
and blasted heath
called
home

row

you know it's funny
I wandered down to the sea
today
such a crisp sunny day
for October
all the deckchairs
put away
for the winter
hints of that coming too
in spitting hissing foam
cold's acoming
to keep you in
sinful wimmin
stay home
don't win
in winter
can't fight
dark nights
in in in
so everyone has to stride briskly
along
except me sitting there humming
my song
of solitude
but they kept rudely
interrupting
my reverie
with their crunching on the pebbles
bunching up together
against the wind
and shouting
all the men
shouting

in all the couples
the man shouted at her
perhaps it's autumn
perhaps these women
are all brooding
but they don't answer
back
and the sounds of men
shouting deafening
louder than usual
whole crowds of them
seem to be here
leering and peering
and shouting
yet it's only a few
one or two in fact
while the women
make a tacit pact
of silence
against the waves
that's no way to behave
in 1991
like slaves obedient
passive
or did I miss something
hidden away
a hermit
if so
it's time to get out
change this
and shout
too

bedrock

important
egos
need sops
flip floppy
malleable
amenable
people
to top them up
with support
all the time

ironic
such towers
needing pit props
isn't it

smug

complacency's
a disease
blasphemy of
utter ease
ignoring
who you please
time and motion
total freeze
as humans
cease
to care

mythology

a word to the lads
and the fables and fads
created by that generation
of men
who ran away
from the working class
you find them everywhere
controlling media
making films
writing books and poems
feeding the myth
of a glorious home
they left behind
stories of a wonderland
of worthy humankind
romanticising
ignorance
as primeval innocence
and it's swallowed
wholesale
by middle class lefties
full of guilt
and gullible nonsense
and handheld cameras
to this beloved reality
of slime
a new sublime
trendiness
instead of the crime
against humanity
that poverty is
has always been
this is obscene
nonsense
for women

pernicious too
haven't you heard
about the vicious nasty
narrow bigotry
how could you
that culture's true
to its menfolk
yet how dare
you not know
that these backwaters
eat women alive
while men thrive
on their mutilation

your song's
all wrong
sonny
there's no lovely
decent community
to long for
they're cesspits
of misogyny
and racism
and philistine swine
a teeming smelly
underbelly
that needs blowing apart
exploding
get-yer-tits-out-for-the-lads
proper exposure
before we can start
on any new
alternative

salt of the earth
gives only
coronaries

'realist' artist

romanticising dirt
hurts only
the dirty
you know

not
the muckspreaders
at all

doubt

how can a socialism
that reveres
working class men
as heroes
be dear
at all
to women

dinosaur

turgid dirge
the T.U.C.
you emerge
a mockery
not a surge
of solidarity
not an urge
to militancy
just a splurge
of ringing
singing
rude
crude
platitude
rotund
profundity
grotesque
complacency
manful
vanity
smug
inanity
saviour
of humanity
you ain't

knots

send me
my alimony
I hate you
for it
this child
I bore it
for you
and love
and heaven above
god knows I've paid
oh who'd get laid
be not afraid
the child
ignores it

interest

do you like
complexity
vivid in intensity
screaming its
immediacy
vast in its
immensity
or do you
prefer
inanity
of bland banality

perch

top dog
human bog
hard slog
to stay
up there

information

yellow pages
stuck for ages
moneyed sages
greedy rages
capital
how you rattle

prospect

how borin'
the whorin'
is done
no longer run
no storing
of fun
for
sage
old age
that adage
has come

routine

lack of chances
mean and wilting
circumstances
uncompromising
daily dances
desecrating
true romances

listen

hark
our lark
is soaring now
roaring how
after dark
light a spark
make our mark
hear him bark
unravel
our travel
marvel
in our
glory
new story
bedevil
his monopoly
of history

tussling

struggle
where would I be
without you
could
clout you
flout you
rout you
but
don't doubt
your fond
return

gloom

felled by depression
it will lift
let it pass
and see it shift
focus action
mustn't drift
alienation
see the rift
self and others
all adrift

torn

her stealing
blank canvas feeling
reeling
as contradictions
vile afflictions
dire addictions
took their toll
tired soul
little role
in the vast
past
scheme of things
featuring
in other people's
paintings
fainting
bewildered
filtered
through years
tears
of sacrifice
weary vice
vicious price
no advice
in confounding
boundaries
floundering for
definition
rendition
small part
troubled tart
tickled
prickled

by crucifying
conflicts
of the heart

invitation

don't be
a lemming
stemming
from
insecurity
of masculinity
divinity
so strong
and wrong
not long
now though
exposure
due
come along
you'll
see

reduction

so now you say
feminism's
wimmin's revenge
of ugly sisters
that bold brave
misters
like you
didn't date
in '68

rejected
we hectored
and harried
and still unmarried
we're all replete
with vengeance sweet
while your defeat's
still due

consciousness?

my old comrades
renegades
of '68
flashing
past famously
dangerously
exalted
these days
who pays
now
music's
halted
whose
days
at the
altar
of acceptance
falter
now

crawl

look forward
to your
back yard
posh patio
you call it
long way
from the mardy
kid
full of lard
fighting hard
to leave us
all
behind
unwind
you're there
stare
a little
not so brittle
mustn't care
so much
about the
vast
past
its vicious
pace
awful
race
lasting
embrace
you're
full of grace
now
but keep your

human face
son
else
I'll
run
back
to my
garden
it's always
fun
there

deception

have a natter
idle chatter
inane patter
doesn't matter
women's
troubles
bubbles
business
prisoners
of smattering
incidents
only

praxis

but how would
an ineffectual
dialectical
intellectual
really know
guts and glow
of real struggle
boil and bubble
toil and trouble
steam and passion
compassion
won't do

lies

ranting
canting
slanting
propaganda
slander
pandering
to greed
insistently
pleads
perverted
subverted
distorted
feeding
lies
ignoring
cries
heeding
only
grander
ties
of power
bleeding
everyone's
hour of
need

thick skin

what kind of school
created this arrogance
this indifference
to other people's
circumstance
this monumental
stiffening
of upper lips
and thickening
of spineless torsos
gruesome war sores
fighting for
right to more
of everything
that power
can bring

it's sickening
Super Sillity

solidarity

in our small separate
desperate
oppressions
should be
the knowing
overflowing
unity
of common humanity
whose sanity
is running out
flouted
routed
clouted
bruised and battered
earthly shattered
shouting
smatterings
of truth
only

and
locked and lonely
in my female
ghetto
I wince
at this evidence
of you suddenly
enemy
revealed
congealed
before
in all that
revolutionary

roar
of liberation
for all

why these
mad mean
stone walls
between us
then
as it
turns out
again
confined
to men

p.c.

you're so wired up
with right on
nonsense
it's tiring
just hearing your voice
no choice
when you phone
but to listen
to the droning
dry political rectitude
pouring out
boring
decrepitude
corsets of attitudes
for everything
that dares to happen
no stone
left alone
in case it
rolls away
uncontrolled
chuckling

worthitude

sisterhood
brotherhood
misterhood
doing good
collectivities
hissing
oughtta
oughtta
oughtta
but
political
correctitudes
are servitudes
surely

deluded

stop being a victim
Gloria
but I like him
when he hits you
black and blue
but I need him
and shits on you
when you screw
but I want him
even bit you
when you blew
only kisses
near misses
frail hisses
bloody blisses
leave him
heave him
away

irena

oh irena
dear
disdainer
of malice
your chalice
flooding now
wounded cow
battered
don't bow
to violence
he'll repent
passion spent
return to vent
even more
manly store
of bloody gore
humble whore
take
no more

leveller

melancholy day
just chatting away
Maria says gleefully
stirring her tea
it's nice
being middle aged
and mouldy
and ugly
no really
don't matter
so much
good looks
and fucking
and lust
and loving
now
the beautiful ones
have caught up
with me
can't feel superior
see

jane

never get over it
you'll learn
to yearn
and burn
and spurn
yet again
dear jane
quite plain
in rejection
not perfection
after all
the marriage stall

stone

you're not listening
again George
how can
we forge
a relationship
if you insist
on all
this mist
dishonesty
misogyny
alacrity
at departure

worm turn

he's running
after young girls
again Pearl
what shall I do
the humiliation
the pain
I'm not vain
but I need
a bit of remaining
admiration
in a marriage
it shouldn't be
administration
of his home affairs
while he's in lairs
all secret
and succulent
a bit of juicy
young cunt
I heard him say
one day
was affronted
the way they talk
about us
but as usual
balked
at exploding
so I look
in the
mirror
at my middle aged
corroding image
and imagine

pastures new
but how to do it
do anything
with such low
unredeemable
self-esteem

what to do
don't stew
in that one
get out
have fun
run away
kick your heels
see how
really young
you feel
when away
from
ageing
effects
of wedlock
learn to shock
and steal
and sin
and win your own
admiration
and give in
to temptations
and thrills
and grow old
disgracefully
and make him pay
the bills

plea

don't join
the antics
of the frantics
stay romantic
and free

family

mum phoned
sounded
small and worried
dad phoned
sounded
hot and flurried
wot curried
common sense

forever female

I'm forty
today
how naughty
you say
loopy display
to pursue
you
like first
flush of dew
rushing
round and round
the bedroom
just like
honeymoon
hot flushing
soon
better give
way
dog day
bitch's
high noon
coming soon

whose crime

very cross
at the loss
who's the boss
in burglary
who's the victor
big prictor
bully boys
such noise
pinch toys
of other people
quite dreadful
utterly culpable
yet I know
how slow
days can be
in poverty
and dole
poor soul
after all

misterhood

it's too late
to aggregate
data
about the working class
and talk like lofty
scholarship boys
for all the world
as if women
except your mum
didn't exist
a trap
a trick
of misogyny
comes with
the prick
this ignoring
underscoring
women
in your glorifying
romances of home
wherever you roam
it's always that
warm and wonderful
womb
to remember
that got you on your way
dear mum
saying always
proudly
daily
loudly
deafening
my son is up

and away
it didn't threaten her
your success
as scholarship boy
didn't violate
her values
about herself
and her culture
men were always heroes
after all

but heroines
can't win
didn't you know
in
these innocent havens
of community
didn't you care
that your sisters
were eaten alive
for daring
to strive
to be different
from the tight
little lives
that womanhood
meant
how many messages
to us
the scholarship girls
have you sent back
with the sentiment
nostalgia
nausea

has the little lass
a space
reserved too
round your middle class
dinner tables
in your fast food fables
of hallowed places
of birth
has she a worth
a value
when you wallow disgracefully
in your dear
beloved origins
that were merely
narrow and nasty
to us
no
it's his and hers
not us
you liars
omission
is worse than sin
you know
a foe
a misterhood
so low and snivelling
you don't
deserve
sisters
at all

ambivalence

the name of
the game
of living
for the end
of the millennium
will be a way
of forgiving
befriending
accepting
acclimatising
our confusion
shedding all
illusions
of certainty
admitting
pain and pleasure
in a single moment
which history won't
solve
resolve
or decide
for us
contused up
and struggling
and juggling
options
concoctions
contradictions
and teetering on
precipices
all the time
a sublime
ambivalence

a constant sense
of tension
and dense
insistent
doubt

hope

you never know
what's in the post
always give it
a ghost
of a chance
to be different
better
tomorrow
no matter
what
your sorrow
today

life

reading
writing
thinking
fighting

life's
inviting
litany